RECORDS OF AN INCITEMENT TO SILENCE

Gregory Woods was born in Egypt in 1953, and brought up in Ghana. He is the author of *Articulate Flesh: Male Homo-eroticism and Modern Poetry* (1987), *A History of Gay Literature: The Male Tradition* (1998) and *Homintern: How Gay Culture Liberated the Modern World* (2016), all from Yale University Press. His essay collection *The Myth of the Last Taboo: Queer Subcultural Studies* was published by Trent Editions (2016). In addition to his six main poetry collections, all with Carcanet, chapbooks of his have been published by Shoestring Press and Sow's Ear Press.

Woods has two doctorates from the University of East Anglia (1983, 2006). He began his teaching career at the University of Salerno in 1980. In 1998 he became the first Professor of Gay & Lesbian Studies in the UK, at Nottingham Trent University, where he is now Professor Emeritus. He is a Founding Fellow of the English Association and has held two Hawthornden Fellowships (1999, 2008).

RECORDS OF AN INCITEMENT TO SILENCE

Gregory Woods

CARCANET POETRY

First published in Great Britain in 2021 by
Carcanet
Alliance House, 30 Cross Street
Manchester, M2 7AQ
www.carcanet.co.uk

A CIP catalogue record for this book is
available from the British Library.

ISBN 978 1 80017 128 2

Book design by Andrew Latimer
Printed in Great Britain by SRP Ltd, Exeter, Devon

The publisher acknowledges financial
assistance from Arts Council England.

CONTENTS

Part One

Part Two

for David Shenton
in memory of John Griffiths

PART ONE

THE ENIGMA OF SURVIVAL

The fittest, who survives, seeks no reward
but rest from mortal combat's melodrama.
By plighting his devotion to a sword
and delegating feeling to his armour,
anaesthetised by neat adrenaline,
he barely feels the piercing of his skin.
He need not even be the pluckiest
so long as he remains the luckiest.

The fittest, who survives, tries to conceal
his wounds, as if they suppurated thought.
Detached from the beliefs for which he fought,
a guilty conscience his Achilles heel,
he sways above the body of his rival,
upbraiding his own heart for its survival.

1

I woke in the night and struggled to find
the light switch, my glasses, a pen. I wrote:
> *It was as if all sounds*
> *and smells were smells and sounds*
> *of you.*

I kept looking back. Did I not want to leave?
Did I already regret the journey I was embarking on?
Did I fear I would never pass this way again?
Was I expecting someone to appear on the quayside
to wave me away or call me back?
I wrote only sonnets.
They seemed to fit the shape of my complaint.

2

A truck was broken down at the side of the road,
its cab folded forward to expose the steaming engine.
The driver was crouching with his eyes shut
in the low shade of a banana tree.

3

For several years I lived in a city in the South.
Its people had a reputation for great warmth.
The climate of the gulf it clings to
had given them every reason
to be open-hearted and optimistic.
The furtive corruption of their officials went unremarked.
There was a uniformed guard with a submachine gun
at the door of every bank.
All was for the best.

In those days we were young. What we learned of the world
we thought we were creating. We often looked for ourselves in mirrors.
We tested our edges against other surfaces.

4
The only trace of previous passers-by
was that of their roadside defecations,
coils of remorse, offloaded with relief,
coprolites to be picked over
by fossil-hunters millennia hence.

I ate the last of my bread before walking down into the village.
Where I had expected hostility my arrival was met with indifference.
I was the invisible traveller so often to be seen
in places no one visits without reason.

5
The annual tribute exacted by the Sovereign
was a single pebble from each province.
The regional governor was expected to deliver it
in person in dress uniform, but otherwise
to add nothing by way of embellishment.
A symbol was enough. The pebble represented the land.

There had been an attack. A plume of black smoke
hung over the commercial district.
We were diverted before we could enter the city.
Men in unrecognisable uniforms waved us off the main road.
Much of the outlying plain had been turned into a refugee camp.
Dark figures were huddled under sheets of tarpaulin and plastic.
Life smelt of excrement.

6

I waited at the level crossing for a train to pass.
It was carrying soldiers to the front.
Leaning out of the open windows, they waved
and shouted patriotic slogans.

On second thoughts, these may have been obscenities,
both gestures and words.
I had waved back, in cheerful solidarity,
but must have seemed an idiot.

7

Back in my hotel room, I sat down at the desk and started a poem,
writing on hotel-headed notepaper with the free hotel pen –
> *Forgetfulness prevails*
> *in these contested forests*
– but I was hungry and dirty. I ordered some sandwiches
from room service. When the boy delivered them I was freshly showered,
wearing only a towel. We gaped at each other but missed the connection.
I ate in front of the television.

I felt I was in the wrong place. The wrong time. The wrong life.
One night a policeman asked me, not who I was
but who I thought I was. It was as if he knew better.
I showed him my papers but he seemed unconvinced.

8

I was waiting at a crossroads for a bus
rumoured to pass there from time to time.
The sandpaper gales of the previous day had died down
and a mackerel sky was filtering the worst of the heat.
The milestone I was sitting on gave a reassuring feeling of permanence.
Distance was precise, as easily measured as time.

The council workers were on strike.
For weeks rubbish had been piling up in the streets.
No amount of disinfectant could sweeten the pervasive odour of death.

9

The gulf was full of rusty hulks, merchant ships
belonging to companies that had gone out of business in the latest slump,
oil tankers fallen victim to the latest OPEC cut in the supply,
even warships, stripped of their ordnance,
too decrepit to be worth selling on
to even the most desperate of banana-republic navies.

10

The priest had none of the complacency of his tribe.
His face was scored with anguish.
Maybe he had just taken one of those confessions you hear of
– a murder or the rape of a child, not yet committed but about to be –
and was being gnawed from within by the rat Indiscretion.
Or perhaps, poor fellow, he had simply heard that his mother had died.

11

The town hall having been put to the flame
by an aggrieved mob,
when I went to have my papers stamped
I was directed to the grandest local hotel.
Its top floor, an open belvedere,
had been requisitioned as an office by the commune.

Two rows of typists, sideways-on
to the view of the mountains beyond the lake,
faced the desk of their supervisor,
which rejoiced in its aptly raised status
on a creaking wooden dais.
If there was birdsong – and there must have been –
it was drowned out by their clacking racket.

As I waited in my suppliant pose
at the feet of the desk, I imagined all those young women
were typing out the names of incendiaries.

12

My beard by now was white and stiff with rime
and my fingers were trembling. I hunched and shuffled forward
as if against an obstinate wind
but the air was stiff and still. Even my shadow was cold.
There was a uniformed guard with a submachine gun
at the door of every place of worship.

13

I visited the bath house. I sweated out the week's events
and a boy with a strigil scraped me clean.

Was I dreaming? An unearthly glow seemed to emanate
from the city, or from under it, as if all
of its buildings were floating on a lagoon of magma
or as if all of its basements were on fire.
Had some effect of the dawn been projected there
from above those clouds
draped over the rooftops like a thick canopy?

14

I changed my identity. In those days it was easy enough.
Typewriter, scissors, glue, approximate photograph.
Leaving the hotel the next morning,
I added a slight swagger to my gait.
It seemed apt to my new past. (The things I remembered!
The tales I could tell!) In no time I reached the harbour gate.
Striding up to the official at the barrier,
a uniformed woman with a clipboard,
I spun a yarn about my accreditation and my duties.

15

I wrote:

> *The last I saw of you*
> *was when the lights had all*
> *gone out...*

16

I often spent an evening walking out
along the road beyond the edge of town,
my only company a thoughtful dog
I'd given shelter during the bombardment
and now could talk to since we shared a past.
We often walked along the railway line
as if to catch a scent of somewhere else,
some distant terminus with no beyond,
a feast of spice and liquefying loins.
Content to speculate, we'd sniff the air
with equal appetite but no resolve.
Reliant on each other's cunning, we
imagined other possibilities,
a trail of other scents to other ends.
In those days nobody believed in love:
its inconvenience disrupted systems
and its sublime expression tore the sheets.
We thought ourselves objectively immune.
The only body that remained to me
was hers, the dog's – her warmth, her hunger and
the way she kicked my ribs while having nightmares.
She listened when I read my poetry
but seemed to like it better when I stopped.

THERE

He travelled to a land
beyond it all – the sea,
the mountains, most of time –
in part to generate
some feeling for this place
he'd left, affection for
this island damning him
to nationality.

From there, that distant land,
he thought of what he'd once
called home, and called it by
the other name, the one
the foreign language used
to speak of somewhere else.

ALAS ALAS

The one renowned for strength
is paralysed by grief.
He drags his feet around
the island, calling for
the boy. His throat is parched,
his voice increasingly
bewildered. Local sights
have failed to catch his eye.

The muscles turn to flab,
his famous sureness in
adversity to vagueness
and indecision. Home
means nothing any more.
The ship has sailed without him.

BLINDFOLD

He whistled up to where
his friend was sleeping but
without effect. He tried
again, imagining
that shaggy body splayed
across the bed, inert
but twitching, deaf to all
but its unconsciousness.

He knew that room. He could
have found his way around
it blindfold, but he failed
to picture this: the friend
was lying there, but not
asleep and not alone.

BEACH SCENE

There's a sequestered place
between the railway line
and the phlegmatic sea,
a narrow beach of rocks
and flotsam. Men arrive
here one by one to share
each other's cigarettes
and silent company.

When the express goes by
with sudden vehemence
they never run for cover
but carry on. And from
the train, subliminal –
a flash of the obscene!

ART IN HEAVEN

The gods look down on you.
They see your sketchy flesh
alleviating the
monotony of time,
reflecting love, and sneer
at its mortality.
That runnel of your sweat
from collar bone to navel!

They think of you as botched,
a pretty good idea
disfigured in the detail –
for they expect perfection,
all ambiguity
resolved to certainties.

JOY IN HARVEST
for John Goodridge

At sundown shrilling swifts leave vapour trails across
euphoric ruddiness. Behind its stalwart horse
the dray processes as sedately as a hearse,
exhausted mourners following at walking pace.

As if the landscape had a duty to seduce,
the winding lane alleviates their sacrifice.
A grassy bank, a mug of ale – such charms nonplus
their weary senses, lavish where their pay is sparse.

One farmhand wanders homeward from the public house
not even having found a soul-mate, lad or lass,
to mark the date with the denial of a kiss.

Acute with ardour and regret, his throaty voice
does nothing more ungracious to disturb the peace
than caterwaul to all the world, Largesse! Largesse!

WOW

The likes of me could not
have anything to say
to you, or nothing but
a stammered compliment,
a thrown-up *Wow!* between
two solid silences.
And what but silence could
you shape in your reply?

The likes of you – you have
no like! – must think the world
a tongue-tied echo chamber
of single syllables,
the rest of us a herd
of inarticulates.

AN IMMIGRANT

We met each other in
reflection, side by side.
While I was waiting he
was being shaved, and when
he'd paid he stared at me
before he left the shop.
The barber called him yet
another immigrant.

I found him in the bar
and took him up to where
I lived. He turned away
to strip. His anecdotes
were innocent and his
erection smelled of soap.

CITY OF LOVE

You left the city. I
decided to stay on.
The faces were familiar,
the buildings even more so.
It was as if all sounds
and smells were smells and sounds
of you: the trams, the sirens,
drunken laughter, breaking glass...

I'd not have been surprised,
revisiting the bench
where we first met, to find
a label screwed to it:
The British poet Woods
ejaculated here.

INTELLIGENT DESIGN

A chapel made of mud
was soon surrounded by
mud huts, a beaten path
from all the compass points,
a space for commerce and
a jetty on the river.
From mud to wood to stone,
from path to lane to highway.

When candles set the thatch
alight it was replaced
with shingles. Domes and towers,
stained glass and buttresses.
A blessing on your spears,
grenades and atom bombs!

HOMECOMING

In mufti he went back
to where he'd spent his boyhood,
the sandstone farmhouse, now
a bed-and-breakfast. When
he reached the bottom of
the lane the dog, despite
its blindness, spotted him
and crept towards the gate.

But when he got there the
old woman shouted from
the door and raised a fist.
His heart contracted as
he'd trained it not to. Chastened
he turned his back on her.

COMPANY

He walks around the city
at night, available
to all approaches, his
unbuttoned shirt a mere
suggestion of diversions
on offer to the bold.
His love of company
is what delivers him.

When he goes home to bed
he dare not go alone.
Like all his meals, his sleep
demands a quorum of
at least a pair. This need
of company defeats him.

HIS NAME

I say his name again
as if within his hearing
a thousand miles from here
a decade in the past
expecting no reply.
He smiled when named, and went
on reading – Graham Greene,
the *Iliad*, whatever.

And having said it, heard
it said, allowed it to
disperse like cigarette smoke
across the room, disperse
and then go stale, we hear
his absence, then as now.

INVISIBLE

He walks around the city
at night without a route
or destination, glad
to see the darkened windows
and hear the breathing silence.
Stray dogs investigate
his boots, but otherwise
he may as well have vanished.

When he goes home to bed,
exhausted but relieved
to have endured, the sun
picks out his nakedness
(the shutters not quite shut)
for envious attention.

LATE SKIRMISH

A bridge. A blessing. Gunfire.
Preposterous, the way
those women stand and stare.
Does God exist? Go ask
them that and see them scatter.
The clouds come down from up
and rain on us. A lorry.
A thunderbolt. The flag.

Too much gets said about
reality. Pipe down.
Let matters take their course.
The dog is laughing. Demons
are sharpening their teeth.
Alas, the bridge is down.

OUT OF BATTLE

The helmet is removed,
the breastplate, then the greaves.
Coagulated blood,
but not his own, is sponged
from torso, limbs and face.
A minor cut is bound,
two ewers proffered, one
of water, one of wine.

The feast will be served up
with tales of how he carved
his way to victory.
But down the years the same
bad dream will rouse him to
the same response of terror.

THEIR DECLARATION

This may have been the place.
It may have happened here.
One said 'I love you' and
the other said the same
as if to differ would
expose him as a liar.
This honeysuckle, this
half-rotten bench, this view.

Or were they here beyond
the colonnade, where water
recites its own descent
into the cistern? Does
the place, does any place,
still echo with those words?

VISIBLE

He walks around the city
at night, aware of eyes
as wakeful as his own
that track him even into
the meanest squints and darkest
embrasures. When he has
to piss he turns to face
the open moonlit places.

When he goes home to bed,
elated to have stood
where thousands stood yet to
have filled their empty space,
his nakedness absorbs
the introspective darkness.

WHITMAN AT TIMBER CREEK

On Harry's father's farm
the creek is overhung
by fretted canopies
of hickory. We swim
as if across the seasons
from light to shade and back,
assiduously toning
and tanning our existence.

When Harry comes to bed
I feel the benefit.
He gives me leave to roam
my idle way across
his prairies, peaks and canyons,
my own America.

PARTS

The sputter of dark fur
between his navel and
the waistband of his shorts...
The Adam's apple, agile
with laughter or elation...
His jaw the more abrasive
the later we made love,
his wit the earlier...

What little I remember
of him is not enough
to make a man, but more
than does to populate
the memory. The parts
incriminate the whole.

UP

Here's Frank O'Hara, naked,
electric with ideas,
unable to lie still.
He gets up in the night
and takes a glass of water
to his old-fashioned desk
to type the day's first poem.
The dawn comes up on him.

When Whatsisname, the guy from
the bar, wakes up and asks
'What's up?' Frank answers with
his most unseemly grin,
'The sun, the Dow, my dick,'
and saunters back to bed.

THE COMPANY OF SOLITUDE

He walks around the city
at night, avoiding what
there is of company.
The sound of laughter sends
him in the opposite
direction, seeking out
the rich inheritance
of his standoffishness.

When he goes home to bed
he thanks his ancestors
and household gods for this
engaging solitude.
A narrow bed is wide
enough for fruitful dreams.

ON BALANCE

A life approached its end.
The one who'd lived it raided
his past for evidence
that it was worth the living,
considering its ills.
For every pleasure he
found corresponding pain,
for every gain a loss.

Desire begat disgust,
delight regret, love grief.
Yet nothing he could find
among his enemies
disqualified his lovers.
He'd had to have them all.

THE UNFORGETTING

The spirits don't forget.
Their memories are long.
They spend eternity
preserving ancient slights
and plotting vengeance. Not
a century goes by
without some fresh reminder
of lapsed dissatisfactions.

Because they can't release
themselves from time, they have
no time to haunt the living.
We needn't feel ashamed
of what they think of us.
They never think of us.

ONE BY ONE

I've not forgotten what
you did to me, nor what
you promised and withheld.
I'm not an idiot.
If I was taken in
by you, it was because
your pose was genuine.
The actor was the act.

When I forget you now,
as I so often do,
I do it with intent,
as if erasing, one
by one, the letters of
your once familiar name.

EVEN NOW

When with men's eyes and fortune in disgrace,
I reassure myself that to the wise
a body is a gaudy commonplace,
mere parts: throat, torso, navel, belly, thighs...

Behind a surface we expect surprise,
as in a palace: part each veil of lace
in hope of penetrating to the prize,
the place within the place within the place.

Even your nakedness is a disguise:
when you deploy your undissembling mace,
the mark of your authority, it lies.

For all your artlessness, when we embrace,
your most uncomplicated sigh denies
the face behind the face behind the face.

A HOCKNEY

As boys transpire the poolside differs,
Those whippy boys who coif us
Or serve us their Italian coffees,
Forsaking tee-shirts, jeans and loafers
For bareness, bellies flat as wafers,
Their sweat as sweet as scented reefers,
Dispersed on suffocating zephyrs.

The painter's calm is like a Sufi's.
They torture him in spiteful rough-house,
Eructing jibes as nice as typhus.
But even so, the silly doofus,
He stays. Suffice to say, he suffers!
Like lasers into lakes of sapphires,
They dive, but barely scratch the surface.

TOMORROW

Tomorrow you'll have gone
and I'll be having to
relearn my solitude,
with books and music, pain
and boredom, silence and
the pleasure of my own
elusive company.
I'm looking forward to it.

But what the future most
benignly promises
by way of consolation
is you in retrospect.
I'm looking forward to
tomorrow's yesterdays.

CAVA ABBEY

Vivaldi. Albinoni.
A bit of Bach. The girls
have occupied the two
enormous pulpits like
anemones in vases.
The boys are arm-in-arm,
parading up and down
the aisles, provoking them.

Impartial as the plain
between two enemies,
the audience receives
the music as its due,
while concentrating on
the courtship of the sexes.

DISTURBANCE

He walks around the city
at night, his footsteps sharp
on cobblestones, his thoughts
rebounding randomly
like bats between the eaves.
He whistles to himself
as if afraid of silence
– or unaware of it.

When he goes home to bed
his dreams express themselves
out loud, soliloquies
in which he has no say,
white-water rafting down
the stream of his unconscious.

The dog knows more than I do. She does, I'm sure of it, as sure
    as sure. She wags her tail at the first
        whiff of a breath of air
on which the last, faint note of an old tune that calls her late sire
    to mind dies out and is heard no more. I
        pat her head in the
hope of a lick, or at least one of her grins, but her eyes, short
    though their sight may be, are fixed, as if on
        the shot corpse of a
game bird, on some glint of this or that I can't see but have to
    have faith in if I'm not to feel snubbed for
        the sake of a sop
to my sighs. She's her own dog. No lead could hold her should she opt
    to shrug it off; no fenced yard but has some
        tight gap to squeeze through;
not a boy who goes by but has a word to woo her with and
    a chewed sweet or piece of gum to sink her
        teeth in, all the more
to be prized for the taste of his spit. Were I to do the same
    she'd growl and turn her back, or stake her claim
        to the thing with a
drop or two of piss, with no aim in mind but to show me it
    was not mine. She treats me like that, as if
        she knew – as she does –
that I so miss the man who used to love me but who walked out
    on us both as far in the past as to
        have left her, but not
me, dead to the thought of his charms. Let her but lap at my hands
    and feet as I did at his and I shall
        feel right to join the

world, as if it were the same one he and I once shared, for all
 that it's changed so much for the worse since then,
 what with the looks I
have to put up with from those who don't know me and the wise words
 from those who do. Let me feel her weight on
 my thighs as I doze
off at night, for all the world as if he had come back to me
 and pressed the side of his face to the heat
 of my lap. I would
stroke her, of course, as I would have stroked him. Why should she not be
 loved if he chose not to be? I don't care
 if she, like most of
her kind, needs no such thing. Must we be led by the fact that the
 taste of love is not in the same league as
 that of a mere scrap
of tripe? Are we no less and no more than dogs? You don't waltz with
 a dog: it can't count the beat; nor would it
 want to, want it to
want to though you may. You find you have to waltz all on your own
 while the dog gives you that look it has, the
 one you think makes it
seem as if it's seen the joke. If it has, the joke is a dumb
 one – but that's not the point. What is? Search me.
 These days I lose my
drift as soon as I've found it. Give a dog a grape and it won't
 thank you, but nor will it make much of a
 scene. As I watch her
wolf her mush with that mad glint in her eyes, I see that a dog
 has no eye for art, head for maths, nose for
 wines or ear for verse.
She lacks the least grace or skill I would want in a friend. I know
 I can't do much to change the way these things
 take shape. All I do

is speak or write the truth as I see it, which is made up of
    both facts and lies. So what's new? The world is
        not a row of signs
we pass one by one. If you set out words in a line – *hat, reef,*
    loud, and so on – you have to have more than
        a crude sense of one
thing and then the next, a string of beads or path from post to post,
    not a thing to be seen in the fog left
        or right. For a start,
this word does not have the same rank as that. This verb vies with those
    two nouns for the soul of that thought as it
        speeds past. Win or lose,
each has its own place in the scheme of things. What is my point, if
    I have one? Well, the dog stands for a theme.
        It is not so much
a dog as a theme that barks and shits, eats and sleeps. And yet, oaf
    that I am, I call her a dog. I call
        her by name. I call
her and she comes to me, a ball in her mouth. (Sit!) She drops the
    ball at my feet so that I can pick it
        up and throw it. (Fetch!)
I could throw a stick or some kind of shoe, but the ball is best.
    I might as well live in a hut in the
        woods for all she cares.
It comes down to this: I like to be on my own. At least, I
    like it when I like it but not when I
        don't. I have the dog
with me (Stay!) but I don't need her. I shan't lack her when she goes.
    I'll think of a new theme to take her place,
        here on the bare earth
by the side of the fire, at my feet. But what if on some dark
    day I should gaze up at the sky and think
        my way through a fresh
set of what-ifs? This is the sort of thing I mean. What if she

were not a dog at all but some kind of
        bird, beaked to rip a
shrew to shreds in the blink of an eye? Or not a bird but a
    car with bald tires and no brakes? Or not a
            car but a bug, one
that drains the life out of you and leaves you a mere husk of skin
    and bones in a pool of your own sweat? What
            if not a bug but
a shark, though one with a taste for dry land? What if she could suck
    the blood from your neck by dead of night like
            one of those bats they
film the myths of to scare the dim? Would she do her worst? Do I
    trust her not to? Face facts: give a dog a
            bone and it may bite
your hand. But for all that those teeth are sharp – they draw blood, don't they? –
    the bite is not meant as a shot in a
            war or a sign of
some mood that will last. It is what it is. Dogs do bite, you know,
    just as men do give dogs bones, at least when
            there's a spare one no
one else needs for soup. What does she think of me, if she thinks at
    all? Does the fact that she has no choice but
            to look up to me
mean she looks up to me? When she lies with her legs in the air
    and rubs her back on the rug, am I meant
            to be charmed by her
wiles? Does she dream, poor fool, that I trust her? Dogs do have rights, of
    course, or so we're told. If you prick 'em, do
            they not bleed? They have
a right to life, if not as much of one as the rest of us;
    but more than cats do, and far more than an
            ant. But I could give
her up in a blink of the eye if she so much as whined out
    of turn to give me cause. Take your farts and
            fleas, I would yell at

her, and go as far from here as you can. I won't call you back.
     You'll be too far to hear if I call you,
          but I won't. For all
I care, you can starve in a ditch. When I beat her with a stick
     – as I do from time to time, for my own
          sake as much as hers –
she looks at me as if at a god, her eyes as wide as those
     of a man who has just been shaped out of
          clay and propped in the
sun to dry. If I'm her god, of course, hers is not much of a world,
     with not much to live or die for. But if
          I'm her god, what does
that say of me, the god to a dog? A god and his dog, a
     dog and her god. What a pair! Not a sight
          to make the heart race,
I must say, still less to thrill the spleen. Woof, she says, and I hear
     yes. Woof, she says, and I hear *no*.
          Does it make sense to
speak of her voice? How could it not? I have been scared by a yap
     in the night that seemed to come from some deep
          flaw if not in the
earth's crust in my own skull at least – ripped from my dreams like a child
     from the womb, I have looked up from my bed
          in dumb fear of the
wraith whose yap roused me and have tried in vain to cry out – but to
     whom? Well – to the dog, of course. The voice that
          woke me, the one I
so feared, was that of the one I called to help me. How I have
     to laugh at my own faith in what has since
          come to be called, in
the dull void of my thoughts, The Hound Who Hounds Me! She leaps on the
     bed when she hears by my gagged breath I've come
          back from the death of

my long sleep and she tries to lick my face, but I push her back
　　to the floor, bad dog, bad dog, go back to
　　　　bed – as if she could
know what a word of this meant – and try my best to go back to
　　sleep. Not till the next day do I ask why
　　　　she yapped at me in
the first place. Was that, too, a cry for help? By now she's gone out
　　on her own, ears pricked up, tail high, grin on
　　　　her chops, glint in her
eye, spring in her step (but what in her thoughts?)
　　and I'm on my own in the hut, not at
　　　　a loss so much as
out of my depth in the slough of who I am, the me I am
　　and have to go on to be for the rest
　　　　of my life. (Or do
I, must I, shall I? Tell me that, you who know so much of such
　　things.) Fail me now, gods of the word, and I
　　　　shall have to nail my
tongue to the rim of the void. I used to sit here on this bench
　　in the shade of the tall pine, the sea spread
　　　　out in front of me
like the floor of a dance hall from which all have fled at the first
　　note of a dirge, and I thought of those who
　　　　did not come back from
the East. I would take my friend's hand in mine but not look at him,
　　for fear of what might be shared in a glance.
　　　　He has gone now, like
all the rest of them. But now as then, the dog wags her tail and
　　lays her head on my knee. The smog that hides
　　　　the far side of the
bay grows pink, but night is slow to fall. The bats don't freak out the
　　dog as they once did – she's got used to them.
　　　　Ebb tide strips the sand

bare. Ebb tide drags a man to his wet death. The ebb does to the
neap what rise does to fall. One tide takes him,
the next brings him back,
full of finned life but none of his own. I hold my hand up in
front of my face and trace its lines with no
sense of where they lead.
The dog tilts her head while she looks at me as if to ask, What
next? She seems to care.

A KNOT

for Tim Franks and Peter Scott, 9 August 2014

Protector of all marriages, Demeter,
At this auspicious time of harvest, trim
The golden hillsides till the windrows teeter
And charge your cornucopia to the brim.

But make this wedding supper all the sweeter
With choirs of LGBT cherubim,
Their voices scented to disperse the foetor
Of homophobic spite and petty whim.

Crack open the champagne! Ignite saltpetre!
No artificial war of words can dim
The luminescence of tonight's partita:

Each husband's husband counterpointing him,
Two hearts harmonic in a single metre
As Love recites its every synonym.

PART TWO

NIGHTFALL

From where I sit, with nothing
to do but this, the scene
involves me in its cheap
theatricals. The dusk
has slathered orange slap
across the overacting bay,
while from the south a storm
is stomping into view.

The boats are being hauled
ashore, and girls who've spent
their spare time flummoxing
the boys are scattering
across the square, pursued
by whirligigs of litter.

WHAT DOES THE POET

for John Lucas

What does the poet imagine you think of him,
draining his consciousness onto the page as if
having developed a leak in the thalamus?

Do you relax with a comforting drink of him,
feeling his thoughts of the world disengage as if
spellbound by lads in the leaves of his Calamus?

Or would you prefer to inhale the whole stink of him,
sweatily goading himself to a rage as if
shouting commands on a trireme at Salamis?

What does the poet imagine you think of him,
feeling his thoughts of the world disengage as if
shouting commands on a trireme at Salamis?

Do you relax with a comforting drink of him,
sweatily goading himself to a rage as if
having developed a leak in the thalamus?

Or would you prefer to inhale the whole stink of him,
draining his consciousness onto the page as if
spellbound by lads in the leaves of his Calamus?

What does the poet imagine you think of him,
sweatily goading himself to a rage as if
spellbound by lads in the leaves of his Calamus?

Do you relax with a comforting drink of him,
draining his consciousness onto the page as if
shouting commands on a trireme at Salamis?

Or would you prefer to inhale the whole stink of him,
feeling his thoughts of the world disengage as if
having developed a leak in the thalamus?

Do you relax with a comforting drink of him
or would you prefer to inhale the whole stink of him?
What does the poet imagine you think of him?

MY SHAME

Restore to me my rib
of femininity,
dear tyrant of a god,
and I shall give you back
your blessed apple, core
and flesh and tawny skin.
Unburn my witches and
unburden my madonnas.

Abandon me to where
you first abandoned me
but let me keep my shame.
Give alms to mollify
my blistered hands and knees
but let me keep my shame.

LOCKDOWN

The mirror captures his
reflection. Honest with
himself (you need no mask
in solitude) he trusts
his own sufficiency.
A single file of days
elapses into months,
the future out of reach.

He has the words, stockpiled
for fear of scarcity,
but dare not draw on them.
They threaten clarity.
Sequestered in himself,
he speaks to nobody.

BLACKOUT

The last I saw of you
was when the lights had all
gone out, the town across
the lake had disappeared,
and I was trying to
remember where I'd left
the torch, oblivious
to everything you'd said.

I saw your silhouette
against the open doorway,
a little darker than
the universal dark.
Of all there was of us
the pain is all there is.

FROM THE LIFE

Creating from the life
a work of art: from this
embarrassed face, this pale
and slightly trembling body,
a two-dimensional
effect of line and colour.
Is this to be confused
with immortality?

The boy has put his clothes on,
gone home and had his supper,
grown up, got married to
his childhood sweetheart and
grown old. The painting leans
against an outhouse wall.

IN DIALOGUE

I lied to him, and he
to me, but nothing we
concealed or falsified
could undermine the facts
and nothing in our voices
had contradicted the
integrity of our
compatible physiques.

Desire's transparency
is more persuasive than
the most articulate
of counter-arguments.
A tongue can say enough
without a thing to say.

RETURN

His exile lasted days –
the years could not engage him.
Nostalgia kept him young:
the orchard where his dog
chased rats, the cleft between
the rocks where boys undressed
to bathe, his mother's smile,
first kiss, first car, first rifle.

So no one recognised
on his return the boy
who looked like someone they
once knew: the velvet cheeks,
the cobalt eyes. Yet he'd
be an old man by now.

ORDERS

Eleven strikes. Then twelve.
The officer consults
his watch. He grabs himself
and rearranges his
insistent genitals.
The cigarette burns down
to his unfeeling fingers.
His men look up to him.

A glare from him could sweep
a whole battalion down
a slope, but all he has
to work such wonders on
are five bedraggled lads.
Their orders are to wait.

VISITORS

He took his boots off at
the door – they shone there like
the noses of a pair
of dogs, exhausted but
alert – and propped his rifle
in the umbrella stand.
He took his jacket off
and draped it on a chair.

She added water to
her soup and brought it to
the boil, then served it with
a pebble of stale bread.
She touched his shoulder when
the partisans arrived.

PRECISION

He's not allowed to smoke
and hasn't had a meal
since yesterday at six.
He waits alone on screen,
not unaware he's watched
and yet above it all,
attention fixed on what,
unsaid, remains unseen.

When all the instruments
are ready bring him in.
Apply the expertise
you judge expedient.
But mind: precision is
the watchword. Find the spot.

NIGHT SCENE

Believable, he lies
across the naked mattress
between his future and
the past. He listens for
a phone call or the door bell,
but nobody relieves
his fruitless optimism.
He might as well be sleeping.

Although his neck and jaw
are bruised, his smile suggests
an easy life, a smile
the naked light bulb meets
with its inscrutable
impartiality.

TRACES

The shutters are wide open,
the door ajar, the mirror
as empty as before
it first caught sight of him.
In here, this is his bed,
and these the very sheets.
His nightmares linger in
their damp entanglements.

His fingerprints have been
discovered everywhere,
all over everything.
Select a souvenir.
The toilet bowl preserves
a smudge of excrement.

BUCOLIC SCENE

The flattened grass is where
they lay together in
the shade of the horse chestnut,
where nothing could be seen
by people on the lane
beyond the hawthorn hedge
or heard by them above
the gabble of the stream.

Just as the stream moved on
from where they bathed in it
before they cycled home
the flattened grass will soon,
like bedding hurriedly
put straight, deny its past.

TRUTH TO LIFE

The youth who's posing for
the figure of himself
regrets the work of art.
He senses a betrayal
in its fidelity.
The more it looks like him
the more he feels he has
to prove himself its better.

The sculptor, referee
and chaperone, gives up.
He turns his back on them,
no longer capable
of telling them apart
or keeping them apart.

TO ARMS

At last the heat has been
defeated by this drizzle,
continuous and silent,
and we can bear to touch
each other once again.
We peel each other out
of sweaty clothes and waste
no time on pleasantries.

You grab my cock, abrupt
with fierce determination
as if to take up arms
in an emergency,
the handle of a sword
shaped to the hero's grip.

VICTOR

His body wields its own
authority. It needs
no camouflage or armour
for self-defence, no gun
to stop the opposition –
he knows exactly how
to cow a man with its
intimidating beauty.

When he inveigles you
into the privacy
of some protective corner
behind a wall or bush
and swiftly bares himself,
he takes your breath away.

ROLL UP ROLL UP

The night has been screwed shut, its padded lining
tight against the restless but immobile flesh.

The streets are dark and all the better for it,
public rights of way in private panoply.

The darkness guarantees complete discretion,
forcing selfhood into anonymity.

The mind is overwhelmed by dreams, a circus
frenzied with implausible performances.

The lion tamer cracks his whip, content to
be both loathed and loved for his authority.

The elephants, adorned as if they needed
more to get them noticed, trundle trunk to tail.

The seals applaud themselves, impertinently
making gentle fun of human vanity.

The clowns annoy the adults with their mirthless
slapstick, foresight meant to look like accidents.

The band is out of tune, its instruments in
disagreement but the beat unanimous.

The clowns are apt to undermine the tight-rope
walkers' concentration, causing them to fall.

The dancing horses throw their giddy riders,
rueful girls in breadcrumbs, rolling in the dust.

The stallions thrust themselves towards the children,
scaring them with intimations of desire.

The mares are more discreet, proceeding sideways,
flanks aquiver, edging into sniffing range.

The nightmare canters round itself, self-centred,
solipsistic, introverted, full of gall.

The sleeper writhes in sodden, tangled bedding,
trapped by wiry tendons, fighting for his life.

The octopus embraces him, consuming
all his energy in its concupiscence.

The night ignores itself, absorbed in other
dark preoccupations, lapped in sleeplessness.

The silence it elaborates is empty,
compromised by all the truths it doesn't tell.

The tiger burning brightly in the forest
lures its victims to the tearful cemetery.

The night withdraws, with obstinate resentment
lingering, a sullen figure at the door.

The morning mist disperses down the valley
like a vague procession of reluctant brides.

The pain is all there is, the pain is all there
is, the pain is all there is, the pain is all.

A BIGGER HOCKNEY

A boy emerges from each ostentatious splash,
Like mawkish baubles, water glinting on his lashes.

The fault-line holds. The air's alive with balderdash.
If surfaces lack moral qualities, he thrashes

The competition with his tan's banal panache,
Defeating anyone his nakedness abashes.

He executes a belly flop that rips a gash
Across the canvas. The computer network crashes.

We leave deposits of desire, like stolen cash,
In random and neglectfully forgotten stashes.

His navel gushes chlorine, but his backside, brash
And trashy, hoards the energy of lightning flashes.

A sunset steals across the smog-screen like a rash,
And dusk subdues itself from melanin to ashes.

ROUTINES

He's moaning in my bed,
apparently disturbed
by an eventful dream,
while on the balcony
I smoke his cigarettes
and watch the city stirring.
The water wagon does
the job of morning rain.

Familiar figures start
appearing, picking up
routines with which my own
may overlap again
today. The stranger in
the bed will leave on waking.

PAST AFTERNOON

A field of Flanders poppies
and celandine. High streaks
of cirrocumulus.
Cascading links of larksong.
We left the car beside
the ruined church and walked
along the hedgerow to
the gate into this field.

We knew we were composing
our own nostalgia, there
and then, in every glance
and every burst of laughter.
This present would become
a past to be relived.

ARRIVAL

He stepped ashore. His voyage
had lasted longer than
the education it
released him from and taught
him infinitely more.
Beyond the harbour gate
the city welcomed him
with pimps and taxi cabs.

The suburbs offered less
but this he took: the church,
the avenue of lime trees,
the gravel drive, the door.
His mother asked him where
he'd been but he'd forgotten.

THE KISS

The bell rings and she's told
to leave. He holds her in
his arms and kisses her,
voraciously severe.
She bends and twists beneath
the force of his insistence
then turns abruptly and
walks out, stilettos clicking.

Back in his cell he puts
his hand up to his mouth
and spits a twist of drugs
into his palm. No kiss
delivered love's reward
with such addictive fervour.

A PLACE IN HISTORY

Forgetfulness prevails
in these disputed forests
where boar and wolves still thrive.
The road between two points
meanders through an era
unvisited by reason.
From every lay-by you
can see the middle ages.

This stone commemorates
events that happened not
a hundred paces from
the spot, a year, a decade,
ten thousand years ago.
The memory is fresh.

LEANDER OF ABYDOS

Leander's lifeless body
responds to every current,
appearing now to wave
at hulls of fishing smacks
and now to test the footwork
of a remembered hornpipe.
His hair seems ruffled by
soft breezes from the hills.

This languid cheerfulness
is nothing like the boy
himself, so muscular,
so single-minded in
pursuit of what he wanted.
Alive, he was unbending.

MAHABALIPURAM

The sea drew back with an
exasperated sigh,
uncovering the city.
It was as if a bed
had been abruptly stripped,
revealing naked bodies
disposed to violate
the most severe taboo.

Yet those who witness such
anathema are turned
to salt. Too thunder-struck
for fear they stood and stared
at those resplendent streets
until the tidal wave.

SUBSTITUTIONS

Exhausted by the heat
and bored with standing still
the statues have gone swimming.
Their places on those plinths
inscribed with fabled names
have been usurped by lads
of rougher tongues and less
forgiving pedigrees.

Now Hector is a punk
with spider's-web tattoos
and needle tracks, Achilles
a racist skinhead full
of paranoid delusions
and Paris just a moron.

THE SHIELD OF THERSITES

My shield is unadorned.
I'm not an easel. Why
should I appease with art
a man who's trying to
eviscerate me? Why
should he get better than
my own compatriots
to whom I turn my arse?

I carry only the
contingent scars of war,
the gouges and abrasions
a military career
accumulates. My shield
must shield me – nothing else.

PREPAREDNESS

They stepped into the last
compartment of the old
funicular and watched
the city open like
a fan. It faded in
the unrelenting sunlight
and shivered, feverish
but stoically enduring.

At the stark belvedere,
they had to hustle change
to use the telescope.
They pinpointed the spot
they would descend to when
their victim was at home.

ENDING

The train is out of sight,
its steam dispersing through
the trees on the embankment.
A whistle sounds before
the tunnel. After that
the valley settles down
to its obscurity
again. The silence throbs.

The one who went away,
the one with the moustache
and epaulettes, becomes
a figment of the past.
The other turns to leave
the station, traipsing home.

OF INTEREST

His private life is there
for anyone to spy on.
A teacup to the wall
is accurate enough.
Surveillance cameras follow
him through the streets and squares
and mongrels sniff his boots
for signs of where he's been.

Who would have thought – and who
but someone with a grudge –
that such a man deserved
such curiosity?
When did humanity
itself become a crime?

PHYSIQUE

His body wields its own
authority and he
submits to it. It leaves
him no alternative.
Its hearty appetites
determine his routines.
Its slightest whim distracts him.
Its illnesses defeat him.

He's never known an hour
of concentrated thought
in which the agile mind
outran the legs. His loves
are always physical,
his lovers always bruised.

A LITTLE DEMON

The laughter? Nothing but
a little demon with
outlandish claws, a foot
at least in length and curved
like sickles. Nothing to
upset yourself about.
His hairy little face
displays a fangy grin.

The boo-hoo-hoos? He's out
to ridicule your sadness
while still eliciting
some sympathy. His tears
are full of gin and onions.
A gesture pokes your eyes out.

THE WARDROBE

The wardrobe looms above
the bed, sarcophagus
of nightmares, silent and
forbidding. Who can tell
how many lives have been
suspended in the darkness
of its infernal gallows?
Whose passings has it hoarded?

To lie here on this sheet
as naked as a flitch
of ham is to submit
to an authority
beyond the touch of reason,
beneath humanity.

MEMENTO

He takes the photo from
his wallet, kisses it
and puts it back. It lies
among the credit cards.
Imagine children, wife
or lover – you'd be wrong.
What he so tenderly consults
is a remembered landscape.

Above a cobalt sea,
steep terraces of limestone.
Among the lemon groves,
precariously balanced,
a dwelling, little more
than where a man might sleep.

RIVALS

Two rivals lead their lives
in parallel, the one
forever conscious of
the other, tailoring
his own achievements to
the other's detriment.
Why, even when asleep
they synchronise their dreams.

Like lands mapped out along a
disputed border, riddled
with landmines and barbed wire,
they formalise their spite
in negatives: I'm not
like him, he's not like me.

ROMANCE

The disenchanted maiden
had no one else to turn to.
The prince, for all his charm,
had been brought up to think
a woman needed beating
if love were to endure.
She gave him back the ring
with which he'd dazzled her.

And so she married not
above her but beneath.
The portly quartermaster's
ambitious son had skills
between the sheets and in
the ways of the black market.

NOT WORTH THE RISK

A day of thunder and
foreboding, finished off
with power cuts. A night
of car alarms, absurd
entanglements and wet
discarded sheets. Before
the morning Angelus
a brandy at the bar.

If you believed in symbols,
you'd spend a day aghast
at its significance.
You'd stop at each event
to crack its code and risk
not taking part in it.

WELCOME

Arrival. Tears of joy.
A seasonal bouquet.
The grocer's premonition.
Brief tour of famous sights;
the suburbs less impressive
but more amenable
to simple human feeling.
Nostalgia. Neuralgia.

A modest welcome speech.
We followed your achievements,
collecting cuttings, watched
the newsreels. Here you are,
at last. The prodigal
returns in hand-made shoes.

NO TITLE YET

The moon, reflected in the oxbow lake
            – beautiful, beautiful, beautiful –
might just as well have been a frying pan
            sautéing phosphorus, given the
distinctly underwhelming shrug at it
            Lady Vanessa was able to
finagle from the depths of her conceit.
            Leaning the whole of her weight on my
reluctant arm, she took possession of
            all but my deepest unconscious, the
forbidding oubliette of my desires.
            Beauty is not in the eye of the
beholder, least of all in eyes like hers,
            bright as they are with self-confidence,
unearned but unassailable. The dues
            people like her feel entitled to!
Her words eluded me, like souls
            fluttering off to oblivion
unnoticed, each accountable for its
            quarantine, artless and absolute.
Empiricism teaches us we know
            more than the sum of our platitudes:
experience is all – so cut the chat!
            Everyone else had gone in from the
parterre to listen to the string quartet
            – Schubert and Dvorak, the mushy bits
with all the instruments in harmony
            even when dissonance might have been
an apter entertainment for the troops,
            Modernist noise to unsettle them.
I hardly knew what I was doing here,

half of me listening heedlessly,
the other concentrating on the night,
            searching the darkness for nothing as
substantial as a unicorn, while she,
            she of the voice like a fire alarm,
kept grabbing me to stake a claim on me,
            hand on my sleeve like a manacle.
I yessed at intervals to keep her sweet,
            no-ing at others to ruffle her,
but she was deaf to all discouragements.

            Footfalls on gravel announcing the
arrival of the cavalry, I thanked
            those of the deities atheists
are licensed to invoke, and made my move.
            Drunk as a monkey, my rescuer
was Vauncey Chilcott, the psychiatrist.
            Leaving Vanessa behind us, we
meandered up the lawn and went indoors.
            Vauncey was waxing elaborate
on reproductive and digestive themes,
            raising his voice to the mezzanine
while I affected not to understand
            English, or English as Vauncey was
transforming it, in case our hosts should hear.
            Half of me wanted to throttle him
and half to cleave to him for old times' sake.
            (Vauncey and I were an item an
eternity ago, precocious students
            testing each other's testosterone.)
With every step he raised his voice a notch,
            decibel building on decibel,
until he was belabouring the art,
            paintings that couldn't shout back at him,

accusing them of any sin a young
              reprobate might have been proud to have
committed on his way to settling down.
              Heresy! Treason! Adultery!
The most splenetic moralist, the most
              obstinate zealot for censorship,
could not have made a coarser case against the arts.
              Yackety yackety yackety...
His lisp insistently unsissified,
              sibilance slicing through silences
in all directions, he seduced himself,
              Syrinx soliciting solitude,
antipathetic to likemindedness.
              Yackety yackety yackety...
He staggered past the paintings in the hall,
              pointing out failures and forgeries,
but stopped at one, a Poussin with a pigeon
              he was convinced was an aeroplane.
He pressed his ruddy nose against the canvas...

              Tiring of Vauncey's intransigence
though disinclined to interrupt his flow,
              much as I wanted to throttle him,
without a word I left him to his task of
              pecking the paint with a fingernail
and made my way distractedly upstairs.
              Whom should I meet in the corridor
but Slingsby Isinglass, the eldest son,
              heir to the earldom but free as a
serenely cageless bird (no title yet).
              Alcohol governed our destinies
and what there was of my attractiveness:
              Slingsby had taken a drop or two.
He looked me over with a breeder's eye,

waiving his standards to favour me.
The moon that night was not the only thing
Providence handled with negligence:
he lunged at me unsteadily, he lurched,
knot came unknotted, and dressing-gown
swung open like the curtains on Act One,
manhood in selfish soliloquy,
the focus of attention centre stage,
strutting and fretting like Peter O'
-veracting Toole's incarnadine Macbeth.
Used to the homage of speechlessness,
he said what needed saying in one word:
'Here,' he exhaled in my ear as he
reversed us through my bedroom door,
tripped on the rug, and delivered me
across the room, half crushed against his chest,
Hercules lifting Antaeus to
divorce him from the safety of the soil.
(Reader, imagine my diffident
bewilderment at being clocked and plucked,
not so much taken as buccaneered
aback, all timbers shivered, buckles swashed!)
Coming to rest on the ottoman,
he splayed his thews. Momentum did the rest,
landing me slap in the Wonderland
between. The etiquette was understood:
England expects, if you follow me.
I duly did my patriotic duty.
Sculpted by vigorous exercise,
his torso, all the tauter in repose,
staggered my faint sensibilities,
reducing me to licking it, as if
life had no more to be satisfied –
the cat that got the cream, and more besides:

slippery ivory, gleaming with
concupiscent intelligence, the flesh
knowingly grudging its promises.
His organs of communication waxed
profligate, gushingly lyrical
while short on sense. The adam's apple bobbed,
much like a float when the hook has been
mistaken for a glint of sustenance.
Glottal and frottal, nonsensical
tirades connected unconnected words
(Thalamus! Calamus! Salamis!)
that needed meaning as a kiss needs cloves.
Even the blandest of blandishments
came peppered with Tourette's. You'd want
more than the Leipzig edition of
Professor Freud's *Interpretation of*
Dreams to make sense of his rudderless
meanderings, assuming sense is what
buys us our purchase on sanity.
The voice was indistinct at times, but then,
true to genetic inheritance,
assumed the elocution of his ilk,
razor-sharp consonants cutting through
flamboyantly expansive vowels.
Heedless of all his unbosomings,
attending to that massive body's needs,
labouring silently, as is my
laconic wont, absorbed in venery,
I, for my own part, was listening
without commitment, absently involved,
shaping an eloquent muteness to
the thrust of his forthcoming coming forth...
Came not the dawn but the lack of it,
and Slingsby Isinglass was fast asleep,

snoring like Etna with adenoids.
Not Gilgamesh bemoaned his Enkidu
nearly as noisily, half as explosively.
Endymion in moonlight never so
prettily symbolised Drowsiness;
yet I was left to crawl away to bed,
Dignified Silence personified.

*

The house curled round its courtyard, like a dog
settling itself in its basket, but
it shared its silence only grudgingly.
All of its ghosts made appearances:
the headless horseman cantered up the drive,
Meissen was smashed by the poltergeist,
the second earl made noises in the hall,
Enid the parlour maid hanged herself
again, still pregnant after all these years;
even the lachrymose Carmelite
was cornered in the chapel by a cat.
Everyone slept intermittently
and rose at what they thought the crack of dawn.
Breakfast was served with a dollop of
concern by staff who weren't concerned at all,
used as they were to the gamut of
ridiculous complaints from cockered guests.
Over the porphyry fireplace, in
a cheerful Canaletto, Venice looked no
more than the sum of her bank accounts.
La Serenissima had pushed the boat out,
flaunting the best of her qualities:
enormous wealth, seductively sublime.
Cowed in our relative penury,

we bowed our heads and ate our daily bread.
                                Nursing implacable hangovers,
the night before's platoon of revellers
                        carried their war-wounds with dignity,
if not without a touch of the DTs.
                                Cutlery clinking on crockery
made tender music in the skulls of those
                        coping with harrowing aftershocks.
But Vauncey, Vauncey, Vauncey, head in hands,
                        telegraphed utter despondency
without a word. The bags beneath his eyes
                        freighted his every expression with
remorse. A bloodshot eyeball warned me off.
                        (Infidel!) Never again would he
so much as shape his lips to say the word
                        alcohol, let alone purse them to
a glass of it. Although I itched to tell
                        Vauncey my epic of Gilgamesh,
enlivening his cheerless coffee with
                        lashings of breakfast pornography,
the morning after barred the night before.

                                Everything seemed inexplicable.
The rooms you might have thought would catch the sun
                        languished in sullen obscurity,
contriving childish secrets out of their
                        blithely self-evident opulence.
The coffee smelt of toast, the toast of coffee.
                                Mirrors reflected things sluggishly
to slow the clocks that kept their backs to them.
                                Ceilings that should have been resonant
absorbed the human voice like cotton wool.
                                Newton himself would have foundered here,
enacting statutes *contra naturam*,

apples ascending in spite of him.
And yet, and yet, and yet, and yet, and yet,
                somehow reality conquered us.
A sparrow trapped in Vanvitelli's dome
                hadn't a doubt it could soar to the
vertiginous infinitude beyond
                – vanity courting calamity:
instead of roosting on the Saviour's cloud,
                horror of horrors, it found itself
belabouring its wings against the stucco,
                falling to earth in exhaustedness
and being thwacked by Milly Bindle's broom.
                Thus do the souls of the innocent
absorb the lessons of their gravity!
                Vauncey'd been found in the billiard room,
not quite as dead as he appeared to be,
                flat on his face on the Qashaqai,
a chisel like a pistol in one hand.
                Lady Vanessa was salvaged from
the punch-line of the ha-ha with a green
                smear up the back of her cocktail dress,
a broken ankle and a tale to tell.

                As for the milky Endymion,
he'd gone before I woke, presumably
                holding his tongue and his genitals
(the dressing-gown was empty on the floor),
                making an entrance in time for the
arrival of a peerless kedgeree.
                All was as if it had never been
conceived of, let alone put into practice.
                Button your buttons and sanitise
your memories! The weekend at an end,
                nothing remained to be grappled with,

material or philosophical –
        nothing, that is, but the banishment
of guests whose lavish welcome had expired.
        Slingsby was distantly intimate
with everyone, to all appearances
        equally charmed by the lot of us
but just as equally indifferent.
        Clad in the habits of privilege
he showed no sign of having had a past
        other than that of his dynasty.
Convenient amnesia was the game.
        Wielding the grip of Agrippa on
the Gauls, he shook my hand and turned away.
        Such is the measure of courtesy
precisely rationed to departing guests.

        Freed from his terse hospitality,
a bunch of us made good our liberty,
        tight in the passing togetherness
of operational necessity.
        Fragrant festoons of wisteria,
the Darcy-Bingley sisters clung to us,
        seemingly fearful of bees they might
be forced to satisfy if left behind.
        Crammed in the Rolls to the station we
complacently allowed ourselves a song
        (Humpsalum, bumpsalum! Absalom,
my bonny boy!), although the chauffeur seemed
        somewhat begrudging of compliments.
Perhaps he hadn't an aesthetic bent,
        Spirit of Diesel, not Ecstasy.
So then we sang the Internationale!
        Vauncey had settled his headache on
my shoulder, but was coming back to life,

humming along with the rest of us.
There was a whiff of turpentine about him,
            something to do with mortality,
no doubt; or, if not that, with paint on canvas.
            Back in the capital, each in the
suspension of his own intransigence
            (each to his own, as the saying goes),
we went our ways to dread the working week.
            Back to reality, back to the
familiar truths of mortgage and employment,
            bliss in the little concessions a
routine magnanimously grants between
            boredom and boredom, resentment and
resentment, laughter in absurdity,
            laughter in bafflement, laughter in
the gaunt implausibility of laughter,
            wretched hilarity, full of the
embarrassments the language traps us in.
            Bundles of viruses, allergies,
addictions, tumours and neuroses soon
            coddled us in their contingency
and left us in the documents for dead.

DREAM MIDNIGHT

At midnight, one midnight in '72,
I wandered the city with nothing to do.
I wandered the city as if I were dreaming,
The blood in my temples insistently drumming.

The doing of nothing took most of the night,
So slow was my progress downwind of the light.
So slow was my progress I thought I was dreaming,
The blood in my temples insistently drumming.

With nothing to guide me or show me my way,
I knew where I was as if walking by day.
I knew where I was, but I must have been dreaming,
The blood in my temples insistently drumming.

As if an idea had a substance to clutch
I might have been holding you, warm to the touch.
I might have been holding you rather than dreaming,
The blood in my temples insistently drumming.

Bewildered by doubt as my fancy became,
I thought I could hear you saying my name.
I thought I could hear you, but I was dreaming,
The blood in my temples insistently drumming.

In separate places and separate hearts
We blended our voices, exact counterparts.
We blended our voices into our dreaming,
The blood in our temples insistently drumming.

Our throats made the sounds of the pleasures they lacked,
Unspeakable vices delivered from tact –
Unspeakable vices of which we were dreaming,
The blood in our temples insistently drumming.

At midnight, one midnight a long time ago,
I wrote you these verses, but you didn't know.
I wrote you these verses as if you were dreaming,
The blood in your temples insistently drumming.

THE EMPTY HOUSE

A book is open on
the table at the window.
The light is filtered through
lace curtains and the leaves
of the old mango tree.
A breath of scented air
(wood smoke and frangipani)
discreetly turns a page.

It is as if the house
had taught itself to read
but only did so when
the family was out
and there was ample time
for Aristophanes.

FAREWELL

The temperature is falling.
The sun goes down behind
the mountains. Shadows pour
into the valleys like
a sleeping draught. My friend,
I wish you could be here
beside me on this path,
exalted and euphoric.

I had no luck. The world
did not indulge me. Love,
though brief, sustains me still.
I'm walking into darkness
along the grassy path
that ends in lasting spring.

ACKNOWLEDGEMENTS

Some of the poems in this collection were first published in these magazines: *Ambit*, *Assaracus*, *John Clare Society Newsletter*, *Left Lion*, *Long Poem Magazine* and *New Walk*. The two Hockney poems were commissioned by Nottingham Contemporary for their first public event (24 November 2009). Other poems first appeared in these books: John Dixon & Jeffrey Doorn (eds.), *A Boxful of Ideas: Poetry and Prose by LGBT Writers* (Paradise Press, 2016); Tony Roberts (ed.), *Poetry in the Blood: Celebrating 20 Years of Shoestring Press* (Shoestring Press, 2014); Merryn Williams (ed.), *Strike Up the Band: Poems for John Lucas at 80* (Plas Gwyn Books, 2017); and Merryn Williams (ed.), *Poems for the Year 2020: Eighty Poets on the Pandemic* (Shoestring Press, 2021).

Many of the skinny, unrhymed sonnets first appeared in two chapbooks, *Very Soon I Shall Know* (Shoestring Press, 2012) and *Art in Heaven* (Sow's Ear Press, 2015).

I'm grateful to Mahendra Solanki and Tim Franks for their early readings of some of the poems.